HOW TO SMILE

THICH NHAT HANH

**PARALLAX
PRESS**

BERKELEY, CALIFORNIA

Parallax Press
2236B Sixth Street
Berkeley, California 94710
parallax.org

Parallax Press is the publishing division of
Plum Village Community of Engaged Buddhism

Cover and text design by Debbie Berne
Illustrations by Jason DeAntonis
Printed in Canada
Printed on FSC-certified paper

The material in this book comes from previously
published books and unpublished Dharma talks
by Thich Nhat Hanh.

ISBN: 9781952692437
E-book ISBN: 9781952692444

Library of Congress Control Number: 2023945490

1 2 3 4 5 Friesens 27 26 25 24 23

CONTENTS

We have a lamp inside us,
the lamp of mindfulness,
which we can light any time.
The oil of that lamp is our breathing,
our steps, and our peaceful smile.

NOTES ON SMILING

If in our daily life we can smile, if we
can be peaceful and happy, not only we
but everyone will profit from it. This is
the most basic kind of peace work.

A smile can relax hundreds of muscles in your face and relax your nervous system. A smile makes you master of yourself.

The essence of our practice can be described as turning suffering into happiness. The basic method is to be mindful of refreshing and beautiful things in the present moment.

Life is filled with suffering, but it is also filled with many wonders, such as the blue sky, the sunshine, and the eyes of a baby. To suffer is not enough. We must also be in touch with the wonders of life. They are within us and all around us, everywhere, anytime.

RECOGNIZING AND ACCEPTING

If we can recognize and accept our pain without running away from it, we will discover that although pain is there, joy can also be there at the same time.

REGAINING OUR SOVEREIGNTY

During walking meditation, sitting meditation, kitchen and garden work, all day long, we can practice smiling. At first you may find it difficult to smile, and we have to think about why.

Events carry us away and we lose ourselves. A smile can help us regain our sovereignty, our liberty as a human being. Smiling means that we are ourselves, that we are not drowned in forgetfulness.

THE ART OF HAPPINESS
AND SUFFERING

Being able to enjoy happiness doesn't require
that we have no suffering. In fact, the art of
happiness is also the art of suffering well.
When we learn to acknowledge, embrace, and
understand our suffering, we suffer much less.
We can learn from our suffering, and we can
transform it into understanding, compassion,
and joy for ourselves and for others.

OUR SUFFERING IS THE COMPOST

A human being should have the capacity to deal with both suffering and happiness. Both are organic, transitory, always changing. A flower, when it wilts, becomes the compost. Our suffering is the compost that enables the flowers of happiness to grow again. We have to learn how to handle our suffering, just as the organic gardener handles the compost.

THE PRACTICE OF SMILING

There are hundreds of muscles in your face,
and every time you breathe in and out and
smile, tension is released. There's relaxation.
You may ask why you should smile when you
have no joy. You don't need joy in order to
smile; you can practice mouth yoga, and you'll
feel relief right away. Sometimes joy is the
cause of your smile; sometimes your smile
is the cause of your joy. Why discriminate?
Wherever you are, practice breathing in and
out. In time, you will calm yourself and your
smile will become real. When we practice
peace and are able to smile, our peace can
influence the whole universe.

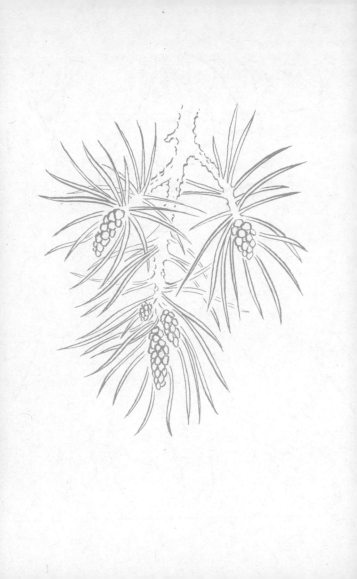

MOUNTAIN PINE

There are pine trees that grow in poor soil
on the mountainside, where there is very
little nutrition for a seed to sprout and grow.
But because of that difficulty, the pine tree
has the chance to go deep into the soil and
become very strong, so the wind can't blow
it down. If the pine tree encounters only easy
conditions along the way, its roots may not go
as deeply and firmly into the earth, and when
the strong winds come, it may be blown over.
Sometimes obstacles and difficulties can help
us to succeed.

BLOOMING LIKE A FLOWER

When we notice the presence of anger, fear, or agitation in us, we don't need to throw them away. We only have to breathe in and out with awareness and embrace the emotion with mindfulness. This alone is enough to calm the storm. Mindfulness is like the morning sunshine on a flower that has closed overnight. The sunshine embraces and permeates the flower, and the flower begins to open. There's no effort. We don't need to wait for a storm before we begin to practice. When we're not suffering, conscious breathing will make us feel wonderful, and it is the best way to prepare ourselves to deal with troubles when they come.

PREVENTING THE
SECOND ARROW

If an arrow were to strike you, you would feel pain. If a second arrow struck you in the same place, the pain would be many times greater. The unwelcome things that happen in life are the first arrow; they cause some pain. The second arrow is our reaction, which magnifies the suffering. We can prevent the firing of the second arrow by simply being present with the real suffering. This allows us to see there are still things to be grateful for, still things that are not going wrong. Happiness is possible immediately, even if everything is not perfect.

WE CAN CHOOSE
THE CHANNEL

A friend once asked me, "How can I force myself to smile when I'm filled with sorrow? It isn't natural." I told her she must be able to smile to her sorrow, because we are more than our sorrow. A human being is like a television set with millions of channels. If we turn awareness on, we are awareness. If we turn sorrow on, we are sorrow. If we turn a smile on, we really are the smile. We can't let just one channel dominate us. We have the seeds of everything inside.

THE SEED OF AWAKENING

Children can see that in each person is the capacity of waking up, understanding, and loving. Waking up means being aware of what is going on in your body, feelings, perceptions, and in the world. Our awakened nature is our capacity of understanding and loving. Since the seed of awakening is there inside us, we should give it a chance. Smiling is very important. If we're not able to smile, then the world will not have peace. It is not just by going out for a demonstration that we can bring about peace. It is with our capacity of smiling, breathing, and being peace that we can make peace.

THE BUDDHA'S SMILE

When I was a young novice, I couldn't understand why, if the world is filled with suffering,
the Buddha has such a beautiful smile. Why
wasn't he disturbed by all the suffering? Later I
saw that the Buddha has enough understanding, calm, and strength that suffering doesn't
overwhelm him. He's able to smile to suffering
because he knows how to take care of it and
help transform it. We need to be aware of the
suffering but to retain our clarity, calm, and
strength so we can help transform the situation. The ocean of tears cannot drown us if
compassion is there. This is how the Buddha's
smile is possible.

MEDITATION IS AWARENESS

Meditation is to be aware of what is going on—in our body, our feelings, our mind, and in the world. Each day thousands of children die of hunger; plant and animal species go extinct; and the nuclear powers have enough weapons to destroy us many times over. Yet the sunrise is beautiful, and the rose that bloomed this morning along the wall is a miracle. Life is both dreadful and wonderful. To practice meditation is to be in touch with both aspects. Please do not think we must be solemn in order to meditate. In fact, to meditate well, we have to smile a lot.

CALMING OUR THINKING

While we practice awareness of our breathing, our thinking slows down, and we give ourselves a real rest. Most of the time, we think too much. Mindful breathing helps us to be calm, relaxed, and peaceful. It helps us to stop being possessed by sorrows of the past and worries about the future. It enables us to be in touch with life and to realize that we have far more conditions for our happiness than we realize.

TOUCHING PEACE

When we sit down peacefully, breathing and smiling, with awareness, we are our true selves, we have sovereignty over ourselves. Practicing meditation is to be aware, to smile, to breathe. The joy of beginning to meditate is like leaving the busy city and going to the countryside to sit under a tree. We feel ourselves filled with peace and joy. What a relief! We can meditate in the sitting position, which offers the most stability, but we can also meditate while we're walking, lying down, standing, or doing things. Meditation can be very informal.

THE JOY OF MEDITATION

In each session of sitting or walking meditation, we can nourish ourself with the joy of meditative concentration by being aware of our breathing, calming and relaxing our body, and touching the conditions that bring us joy and happiness in the present moment. Meditation helps us restore peace, solidity, and harmony in our body so we can suffer less and make progress on our spiritual path. The joy and bliss of meditation sustains us on our path of practice and gives us strength to look more deeply into difficult feelings and situations.

A HALF SMILE

A tiny bud of a smile on our lips nourishes awareness and calms us miraculously. It returns to us the peace we thought we had lost. Our smile will bring happiness to us and to those around us. Even if we spend a lot of money on gifts for everyone in our family, nothing we buy could give them as much happiness as the gift of our awareness, our smile. And this precious gift costs nothing.

When I see someone smile, I know immediately that he or she is dwelling in awareness. This half-smile, how many artists have labored to bring it to the lips of countless statues and paintings? I am sure the same smile must have been on the faces of the sculptors and the painters as they worked. Can you imagine an angry sculptor giving birth to such a smile?

Mona Lisa's smile is light, just a hint of a smile. Yet even a smile like that is enough to relax all the muscles in our face, to banish all worries and fatigue.

BITTER MELON

There's a vegetable in Vietnam called bitter melon. The Chinese word for bitter also means suffering. If you're not used to eating bitter melon, you may suffer. But according to traditional medicine, bitterness is good for your health. Some people call it "refreshing melon," because eating it makes you feel fresh and cool—and it's delicious, even the bitterness.

Suffering is bitter, and our natural tendency is to run away from it. Our store consciousness, our unconscious mind, can set up a program of behaviors to help us run away from suffering and approach only what's pleasant. This prevents us from knowing the goodness of suffering, the healing it can bring. But our conscious mind knows that suffering has things to teach us, and that we shouldn't be afraid of it. We are ready to suffer a little bit in order to learn, grow, and heal. We have to use our intelligence. We use our concentration to get insight, to transform the suffering and become an enlightened one, a free person.

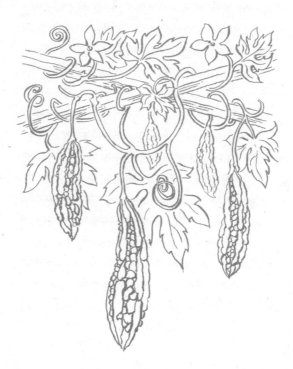

HANDLING AN
UNPLEASANT FEELING

Our feelings play an important part in how
we perceive, think, and act. Buried inside are
painful feelings we may be afraid to bring into
our conscious mind because they'll make us
suffer. Practicing breathing and smiling, we
can be in contact with our feelings and accept
them. If we face our unpleasant feelings with
care, affection, and nonviolence, and mindfully
observe them, our unpleasant feelings can
illuminate much for us, offering us insight and
understanding into ourselves and society.

When we embrace and calm an unpleasant
feeling, we do this for all our ancestors and for
future generations. Our suffering is not only
an individual manifestation, but a collective
manifestation from many generations and from
society. We are not the only one responsible.

TAKING CARE OF ANGER

Anger is not an enemy. Both mindfulness and anger are ourselves. Our practice is based on the insight of nonduality. Mindfulness is there not to suppress or fight against anger, but to recognize and take care, like an older sibling helping a younger one. The energy of anger is recognized and embraced tenderly by the energy of mindfulness. Every time we need the energy of mindfulness, we just touch that seed by means of our mindful breathing, mindful walking, and smiling, and then we have the energy ready to do the work of recognizing, embracing, looking deeply, and transforming. Within the seed of mindfulness is the seed of concentration. With these two energies, we can liberate ourselves from afflictions.

HOUSE ON FIRE

If your house is on fire, the most urgent thing to do is to go back and try to put out the fire, not to run after the person you believe to be the arsonist. If you run after the person you suspect has set fire to your house, the house will burn down while you're chasing them. The wise thing to do is to go back and put out the fire. When you're angry, if you continue to interact or argue with the other person or if you try to punish them, you are acting exactly like someone who runs after the arsonist while everything goes up in flames.

WHAT PART DO WE CONTRIBUTE?

Pain may be unavoidable. But whether we suffer or not is up to us. Birth, old age, and sickness are natural. It is possible not to suffer because of them when you have chosen to accept them as part of life. You may choose not to suffer, even if pain or sickness is there. How you see life and your particular situation depends on your way of looking. If we look deeply into our suffering, we can ask ourselves how we contribute to it. That doesn't mean that our suffering isn't real, just that we can lessen it instead of adding to it, and we can even transform it.

WATERING GOOD SEEDS

One way of taking care of our suffering is to invite a positive seed of the opposite nature to come up. For example, if the seed of arrogance comes up, you can practice mindfulness of compassion. If you practice this every day, the seed of compassion in you will become strong and will come up as a powerful zone of energy. We can selectively water the good seeds and refrain from watering the negative seeds. This doesn't mean we ignore our suffering; it just means we allow the positive seeds that are naturally there to get attention and nourishment. If there are difficulties in our relationships, we practice watering the flowers in ourself and in our loved ones, and we can very well restore communication and revive the happiness we had before.

IN TOUCH WITH MOTHER EARTH

Touching the earth, letting your fingers feel the soil, and gardening are wonderful, restorative activities. If you live in a city, you may not have many opportunities to hoe the earth, plant vegetables, or take care of flowers. But you can still find and appreciate a small patch of grass or earth and care for it. Being in touch with Mother Earth is a wonderful way to preserve your mental health.

With awareness of the Earth's generosity and support, and of our deep connection with her, we can generate a pleasant feeling. Knowing how to create moments of joy and happiness is crucial for our healing. It is important to be able to see the wonders of life around us, to recognize the conditions of happiness that already exist.

NEUTRAL FEELINGS

Neutral feelings are those which are neither pleasant nor unpleasant. With mindfulness, a so-called neutral feeling can become a pleasant or unpleasant feeling; it depends on our way of handling it. For example, when we have a toothache, we know that it would be wonderful not to have a toothache. Yet when we don't have a toothache, we're still not happy. A non-toothache is something very pleasant. But if we're not aware of our non-toothache, we have a neutral feeling. When we practice mindfulness and become aware of our non-toothache, the neutral feeling becomes a positive feeling, a feeling of well-being.

TURNING NEUTRAL FEELINGS INTO PLEASANT FEELINGS

The term "neutral feeling" doesn't seem quite accurate, because with full awareness, neutral feelings can become the kind of pleasant feelings that can be more sound and longer lasting than other kinds of pleasant feelings. Eating good food or hearing words of praise usually gives rise to a pleasant feeling; flying into a rage or having a toothache is an unpleasant feeling. These kinds of feelings usually push us around, and we become like clouds blown in the wind.

Our feelings of peace and joy will be more stable and long-lasting if we know the source of our neutral feelings. The essence of happiness is a body that is not in pain and a heart and mind that are not oppressed by anxiety, fear, or hatred. Sitting in meditation, we can arrive at a stable feeling of joy, realizing the stillness of body and the clarity of mind. We are no longer pushed around by the highs and lows and we enjoy our feeling of well-being.

WHAT'S NOT WRONG

We have to learn to practice touching what is not wrong, inside us and around us. When we get in touch with our eyes, our heart, our liver, our breathing, and our non-toothache and really enjoy them, we see that the conditions for peace and happiness are already present. When we walk mindfully and touch the earth with our feet, when we drink tea with friends and touch the tea and our friendship, we get healed, and we can bring this healing to society.

SITTING IN CALM AND SAFETY

With mindfulness, we become aware of the suffering that's going on around us. There are many who can't sit like us in calm and safety; a bomb or rocket might fall on them at any moment. What they want is peace, a cessation of the killing, but they don't have it. There are many of us who have a chance to sit in much more safety and who live in a situation where this kind of suffering doesn't exist, but we don't seem to appreciate it. Mindfulness helps us to be aware of what's going on around us, and suddenly we know how to treasure the conditions of peace and happiness that are available in the here and the now.

ENGAGED BUDDHISM

When I was in Vietnam, our villages were being bombed. Along with my brothers and sisters, I had to decide what to do. Should we continue to practice in our monastery, or must we leave the meditation halls to help the people who were suffering under the bombs? After careful reflection, we decided to do both—to go out and help people and to do so in mindfulness. We called it Engaged Buddhism. Mindfulness must be engaged. Once there is seeing, there must be acting. Otherwise, what is the use of seeing? With mindfulness, we will know what to do and what not to do to be of help. If we maintain awareness of our breathing and continue to practice smiling, even in difficult situations, many people, animals, and plants will benefit from our way of doing things.

PERCEPTIONS

Many people want to get rid of their painful
feelings, but not of the beliefs and viewpoints
that are the very root of their feelings. After
recognizing a painful feeling, becoming one
with it, calming it down, and releasing it, we
can look deeply into its causes, which may
be based on inaccurate perceptions. When
we understand the causes and nature of our
feelings, they will begin to transform. When we
misperceive a person or an object, we may feel
anger, disappointment, or annoyance. We need
to remember that most of our perceptions are
wrong. Practicing full awareness means to look
deeply and go beyond our inaccurate perceptions, to see the true nature of everything.

AVOIDING MISPERCEPTION

Thinking is at the base of everything. It is important for us to bring awareness into each of our thoughts. Without a correct understanding of a person or situation, our thoughts can be misleading and create confusion, despair, anger, or hatred. Our most important task is to develop correct insight. If we see deeply into the nature of interbeing, that all things "inter-are," we will stop blaming, arguing, and killing, and we will become friends with everyone.

INTERBEING

Our anxieties and difficulties come from our inability to see the true nature of all phenomena. We see their outward appearance, but we often fail to recognize their impermanent and interbeing nature. Everything penetrates and is made of everything else. Everything *is* everything else. No phenomenon can be by itself alone. Everything has to inter-be with everything else. All phenomena have the nature of interdependence.

ARE YOU SURE?

The real meaning of "to be" is to inter-be. You cannot be by yourself alone; you have to inter-be with everyone and everything else. This is true of everything: the flower, the table, the river. You can touch this insight by looking deeply. Touching the truth of nonself, you are free. But if you allow the illusion of self to occupy you, you'll continue to suffer a lot.

Scientifically speaking, the idea of a self, an entity, is an illusion. For example, you say I am Vietnamese, but are you sure? In my case I don't have a Vietnamese passport or identity card, so legally speaking, I'm not Vietnamese. Looking into my writings, my person, my Dharma talks, you see several cultural streams: French, Chinese, Indian, even Native American; there's no such thing as Vietnamese culture. And ethnically speaking, there's no Vietnamese race; looking into me you can see Melanesian, Indonesian, Mongolian, and other non-Vietnamese elements. Each of us has elements of many other cultures and ethnicities. We're not "pure." Knowing this, you are free. The cosmos has come together to help you to manifest. In you the whole cosmos can be found.

MINDFULNESS IN
EVERY MOMENT

There are moments when we're capable of
seeing the interbeing, nonself nature in people
and things. But at other moments we forget
and fall back into our world of imaginary con-
struction. Continuous practice is important
for the flower of enlightenment to bloom per-
manently in the field of our mind. Mindfulness
can transform all our thoughts and emotions;
every state of mind is sensitive to the energy
of mindfulness.

IMPERMANENCE

Although intellectually we know that all things are impermanent, in our daily lives we carry on as though things were permanent. Impermanence is more than an idea; it's a practice to help us touch reality. We can nourish our insight into impermanence all day long; every phenomenon can reveal to us the nature of impermanence. We should learn to be more aware of impermanence. If we're in good health and aware of impermanence, we'll take good care of ourselves. When we know the person we love is impermanent, we'll cherish our beloved all the more. When we practice mindfulness of impermanence, we become more present and more loving. Impermanence teaches us to respect and value every moment and all the precious things around and inside us.

NONSELF

Just as the flower is made of the sunlight, the
soil, the rain, and so on, we know that everything, including ourself, is made only of nonself
elements. Thanks to this realization, we have
the insight that happiness and suffering are
not individual matters. We see the nature of
interconnectedness of all things. We all have
the capacity to live with the nondiscriminative
wisdom that everyone and everything belongs
to the same stream of life.

THE DANDELION WILL
KEEP YOUR SMILE

Our smile will bring happiness to us and to
those around us. Even if we spend a lot of
money on gifts for everyone in our family, nothing we buy could give them as much happiness
as the gift of our awareness, our smile. And
this precious gift costs nothing. At the end of
a retreat in California, a friend wrote this poem:

> *I have lost my smile,*
> *but don't worry.*
> *The dandelion has it.*

If you have lost your smile and yet are still
capable of seeing that a dandelion is keeping
it for you, the situation is not too bad. You still
have enough mindfulness to see that the smile
is there. You only need to breathe consciously

one or two times and you will recover your smile. The dandelion is one member of your community of friends. It is there, quite faithful, keeping your smile for you. In fact, everything around you is keeping your smile for you. You don't need to feel isolated. You only have to open yourself to the support that is all around you, and in you. Like the friend who saw that her smile was being kept by the dandelion, you can breathe in awareness, and your smile will return.

WE ARE ALL LINKED
TO EACH OTHER

Maintaining our awareness of the interdependent nature of life, we know the survival of the developing countries cannot be separated from the survival of the materially wealthy, technically advanced countries. Poverty and oppression bring war and, in our time, every war involves all countries. The fate of each country is linked to the fate of all others. The only way to end the danger is for each of us to recognize each other as brothers and sisters. We are all humankind, and our life is one.

LEARNING FROM SUFFERING

As you look deeply into suffering, you may
find out many things. You can investigate its
roots and see what habits of consumption
you've been feeding it with, what you ingest
in terms of the four nutriments: edible food;
sense impressions (sights, sounds, etc.,
that you bring in through your senses); your
deepest motivations; and your thinking. You
may discover that your suffering is not only
an individual manifestation but a collective
manifestation that carries within it the suffering
of your parents, your ancestors, your people,
your nation, and the world. Maybe your parents
or ancestors didn't know how to handle their
suffering and transform it, so they have transmitted that suffering to you. If we listen deeply
enough, we will understand and suffer less.

OUR WORLD

Many of us worry about the world situation. As individuals, we feel helpless, despairing. The situation is so dangerous, injustice is so widespread, the danger is so close. In this kind of situation, if we panic, things will only become worse. We need to remain calm, to see clearly. Meditation is to be aware and to try to help. After the war, many people left Vietnam to travel in small overcrowded boats across the Gulf of Siam. Often they were caught in storms or rough seas. People could panic, making the boat more likely to sink. But if one person aboard could remain lucid and calm, knowing what to do and what not to do, that person could help the boat survive. Their voice and body would communicate clarity and calm; people would trust them and listen to what they had to say. One such person can save the lives of many. Our world is something like a small boat. Compared with the cosmos, our planet is a very small boat. We may be about to panic because our situation is no better than that of the small boat in the sea. Humankind has become a very dangerous species. We need people who can sit still, are able to smile, and can walk peacefully in order to save us. In my tradition it's said that you are that person, that each of us is that person.

WHAT IS MOST IMPORTANT?

The seed of mindfulness is in each of us, but
we usually forget to water it. We think that
happiness is only possible in the future—when
we get a house, a car, or a degree. We struggle
in our mind and body, and we don't touch the
peace and joy that are available right now in
the blue sky, the green leaves, and the eyes
of a loved one. What is most important? Many
people have passed exams and bought houses
and cars, yet they are still unhappy. What is
most important is to find peace and to share
it with others. To have peace, you can begin
by walking peacefully. Everything depends
on your steps.

WALKING MEDITATION

Walking meditation is to be aware and to enjoy walking. We walk, not in order to arrive, but just to walk—to be in the present moment, aware of our breathing, our walking, and to enjoy each step. Any time I have to go from one place to another, I practice walking meditation—even if the distance is only five or six feet. I do not have any other style of walking—just mindful walking. It helps me very much. It brings me transformation, healing, and joy.

WALKING ON THE EARTH

The Apollo astronauts were able to take a picture of the Earth from far away and send it to us. It was the first time we saw the whole Earth—very beautiful—a bastion of life. With mindful walking, we have a chance to enter into deep communion with the planet Earth and realize the Earth is our home. It's wonderful to enjoy walking on planet Earth. Mother Earth has brought us to life and provided all the conditions for our survival. She has developed an environment from which humans can manifest and thrive. She created a protective atmosphere, with air we can breathe, abundant food for us to eat, and clear water for us to drink. She is constantly nourishing and protecting us. She is our mother and the mother of all beings.

IN THE FOOTSTEPS
OF THE BUDDHA

In 1968, I went to India for the first time. I wanted to visit Bodhgaya where the Buddha reached enlightenment. So I took a flight from New Delhi to Patna, and as we were coming in to land, I had fifteen minutes to contemplate the landscape below. For the first time, I saw the legendary Ganges River and, looking down, I could see the footprints of the Buddha a little bit everywhere. I was very moved. The Buddha loved to walk, and he spent a lot of time walking along the river and visiting the river kingdoms. I visualized the Buddha walking with dignity, freedom, peace, and joy. He walked like that for forty-five years, bringing his wisdom and compassion to many places and sharing his practice of liberation with many people—from the most powerful to the most excluded people in society. There were no cars, trains, or planes. He walked with his friends and disciples and visited and taught in perhaps fifteen ancient kingdoms of India and Nepal, meeting people and helping them to practice. Looking down, I vowed that I would practice walking meditation to bring the steps of the Buddha to other parts of the world. I have been all over the world and have shared the practice of walking meditation with many people. I have friends, both monastic and lay, who have been walking like that on all five continents. The Buddha's footprints are now everywhere.

MINDFUL STEPS

Wherever you are, you can enjoy mindful walking, and every time you make a mindful step you stop your forgetfulness and go back to life, touching the wonders of life for your healing and transformation. It's very nice to walk for your parents or your grandparents who may not have known the practice of walking in mindfulness. Your ancestors may have lived their whole lives without the chance to make peaceful, happy steps. We practice for all generations of ancestors and descendants.

EATING WITH FAMILY
AND FRIENDS

Having the opportunity to sit with our family
and friends to enjoy wonderful food is something precious, something not everyone is able
to do. Sitting at the table with other people is a
chance to breathe and offer an authentic smile
of friendship and understanding. If people
eating together cannot smile at each other,
then something is not right. Look down at the
food in a way that allows it to become real and
reveals your connection with the earth. Each
bite contains the life of the sun and the earth.
You can see and taste the whole universe in a
piece of bread.

MINDFUL EATING

Many people in the world are hungry. When I hold a bowl of rice or a piece of bread, I know that I am fortunate. I feel compassion for all those who have no food to eat and are without friends or family. This is a very deep practice. Looking at our plate, we see Mother Earth, the farm workers, and the tragedy of hunger and malnutrition. Mindful eating can cultivate seeds of compassion and understanding that will inspire us to do something to help hungry and lonely people be nourished.

LISTENING TO OUR
WOUNDED CHILD

Inside each of us is a young, suffering child.
We've all had times of difficulty as children
and many of us have experienced trauma. To
protect ourselves from further suffering, we try
to forget those painful times. But the wounded
child is always there, calling for our attention.
We have to go back to tenderly embrace and
listen to the child inside. We can talk to the
child with the language of love, saying, "My
dear, I know you've suffered. I've neglected
you. I'm sorry. I won't leave you alone again."
If you go back to the wounded child and listen
carefully every day for five or ten minutes,
healing will take place. When you go on a
walk, contemplate the sunset, or climb up a
beautiful mountain, invite them to enjoy it with
you. When sitting alone, you can talk to your

wounded child, "My darling, I know you've been seriously wounded. But we have grown up now. Take my hand and let's walk out of the past into the present moment." Our sangha can help. We can help each other be released from the prison of the past or the future. Although I received love and care from my parents, I too have done this practice, and it has helped me tremendously.

RESTORING COMMUNICATION

Our ancestors may not have known how to
care for their wounded child within, so they
have transmitted their wounded child to us.
Our practice is to end this cycle. The people
around us, our family and friends, may also
have a severely wounded child inside. If we've
managed to help ourselves, we can also help
others. When we've healed ourselves, our
relationships with others become much easier.
There's more peace and love in us, and we can
allow people to love us. Before, we may have
been suspicious of everything and everyone.
Compassion helps us relate to others and
restore communication.

A STORM OF EMOTIONS

Many young people have difficulty handling strong emotions and they suffer a great deal. Some commit suicide because they have no other method for dealing with strong emotions than putting an end to their life. Emotions are like a storm; they come, stay for a while, and then move on. We shouldn't die because of an emotion. Parents can teach their children how to handle their emotions and weather the storms more easily. When we have a strong emotion, we are like a tree in a big storm. We don't stay up in our head, in the high branches that are tossed about by the wind and could be broken off. Bring your awareness down to your abdomen, to the trunk of the tree, which is stable and rooted. Become still, not carried away by your thinking and emotions. Practice deep breathing, breathing down into your abdomen. It isn't difficult. Teenagers and children can learn it. We shouldn't wait for strong storms to arrive before starting the practice. If you practice together with your child, for five or ten minutes each day, for two or three weeks, the practice of deep belly breathing will become a habit. When the emotion is about to come up, the young person will know what to do. They will have the experience of knowing they can survive their emotions.

CHILDREN NEED OUR UNDERSTANDING

When we look deeply into our children, we see all the elements that have produced them. They are the way they are because of our culture, economy, society, and because of the way we ourselves are. We can't simply blame our children when things go wrong; many causes and conditions have contributed. If parents practice mindfulness and compassion in their daily lives, children will naturally learn from them. Listening deeply and using loving speech, you can water the good seeds in children. When we know how to transform ourselves and our society, our children will transform also.

DEPRESSION

Embracing our suffering may seem to be the opposite of what we want to do, especially if the suffering is very large, as with depression. Depression is widespread in our time. It can take away our peace, joy, stability, even our ability to eat, move about, or do simple tasks. It can seem insurmountable, and we may think the only thing we can do is either run away from it or give in to it. But recognizing and embracing this great suffering without judgment, the suffering will naturally calm down, and then you will have the chance to look into it deeply to find out why it has come to you. It's been trying to get your attention and tell you something, and now you can take the opportunity to listen. You can ask someone to look with you—a teacher, a friend, a psychotherapist. Whether alone or together with friends, you can explore its roots, and see with what nutriments and habits of consumption you have been feeding your sorrow. You can discover how to transform the compost of this suffering into the flowers of understanding, compassion, and joy.

COMING THROUGH THE STORM

When you don't know how to handle the suffering inside you or how to help handle the suffering around you, you may try not to be there anymore, thinking that will make you feel better. To commit suicide is an act of despair. It's not wise. You think you'll stop being after you die. But that's not true. You continue always, in many ways. The suffering will go on, not only for you but for other people who care about you. If you lose hope, they will lose hope. If that habit energy is in the family, it's one more reason to practice. If we have a good environment, a good sangha, good friends surrounding us, then we have more of a chance to get in touch with the kind of wisdom and practice that can help us. Don't pretend, perhaps out of pride, that everything is okay.

Sit among us and say, "Dear sangha, here is my pain, my sorrow, my despair. Please help me recognize and embrace it. I need the collective energy of the sangha." If you can end the habit energy, you transform it not only for yourself, but for the whole lineage. With that energy of love and compassion, you won't do things that make people suffer anymore. Practice breathing, walking, and recognizing this habit energy in you. Say, "Hello, my habit energy. I intend for you not to be there anymore. You have been my friend for a long time. I'm going to help you." Embrace it, work with it, and transform it. We don't have to fight. We only have to recognize and smile to it. The insight that death and birth inter-are is very important.

UPROOTED

Our society is a difficult place to live. If we're not careful, we can become uprooted, and then we cannot help change society to make it more livable. Meditation is a way of helping us stay in society, and this is very important. Many young people who come to Buddhist practice come by way of psychology, and they look to the practice of meditation to solve psychological problems. Having lived for quite some time in this society, I'm aware there are many things that make me want to withdraw, to go back to myself. But my practice helps me remain in society. I know that if I leave society, I can't help to change it. We need to keep our feet on earth and stay in society. This is our hope for peace.

HEALING FROM
CHILDHOOD ABUSE

As a victim of childhood abuse, you don't want
others to suffer as you have. With a strong
aspiration to help and a determination to practice, you transform yourself into a bodhisattva,
an activist, an agent of peace, and you begin
to heal right away. You transform your suffering
into the kind of insight that will help yourself,
your friends, and society. Practice looking
deeply to see that your parents didn't have a
chance to encounter wise teachings or good
friends. If they had lived in a better environment, they might have behaved differently. This
is true of everyone.

For those of us who have been a victim of
sexual abuse, there is the teaching that the
mud and lotus inter-are; we don't discriminate,

we have to accept both. It is possible to transform the mud into the lotus. Ideas like production and destruction, birth and death, defiled and immaculate, are just creations of our mind. Neither defiled nor immaculate is the teaching and practice that will help us transcend the idea of defilement and impurity. Everything is impermanent, everything changes. You don't have to bear that kind of suffering forever. You make the great vow to become a bodhisattva and, with that deep aspiration, there's much you can do to help protect children, young people, and couples from sexual abuse and sexual misconduct, through education and so on. When your energy of aspiration is strong, you begin to heal right away.

GETTING UNSTUCK

When we feel that we are a victim of someone, we suffer and tend to become passive in our lives. Instead, we can behave positively and take the situation into our own hands. Once we feel sorry for ourselves and feel we're a victim, it's difficult for us to be fully present and to go ahead and do what we want to do. We think we're the victim, but in fact the other person is a victim of their own suffering and ignorance. With mindful awareness, we can come to the wisdom of nonself and nondiscrimination. This insight protects us. Once we're inhabited by this energy and wisdom, we won't suffer anymore, and we won't make other people suffer.

LIVING TOGETHER

When we live with another person, to protect each other's happiness we should help each other transform the internal knots that we produce together. By practicing loving speech and deep listening in order to understand, we can help each other a great deal. Happiness is not an individual matter. If the other person is not happy, we will not be happy either.

If we are peaceful, if we are happy, we can smile and blossom like a flower, and everyone in our family, our entire society, will benefit from our peace.

NON-ACTION

Love and hatred are organic. We can quickly become angry with the one we love, and we can also come to love someone we hated. When we're angry, we can give ourselves a little space by taking some deep breaths. This will prevent us from saying or doing something that we may regret later. We recognize that this feeling of anger is a momentary reaction. Following our breathing in and out, and not feeding the anger with our perceptions, it will calm down and cease. When someone says something challenging, if we can smile and return to our breathing, this will be a living teaching, and others will be able to touch it. Sometimes, through non-action, we can help more than if we do a lot. Remaining calm, we can change the situation.

LOVING SPEECH AND
DEEP LISTENING

All of us have pain, anger, frustration, and we need to find someone willing to listen to us who is capable of understanding our suffering. Before we say something, we have to understand what we're saying and also the person to whom our words are directed. With this understanding, we will not say things to make the other person suffer. Blaming and arguing are forms of violence. If we suffer greatly, our words may be bitter, and that won't help anyone. We have to learn to calm ourselves and become a flower before we speak. This is the art of loving speech. Listening is also a deep practice. We listen in a way that we understand the suffering of others. We empty ourselves and leave space so we can listen well. If we breathe in and out to refresh ourselves, we will be able to sit still and listen to the person who is suffering. When they are suffering, they need someone to listen attentively without judging or reacting. If they cannot find someone in their family, they may go to a psychotherapist. Just by listening deeply, we already alleviate a great deal of their pain. This is an important practice of peace. We have to listen in our families and in our communities. We have to listen to everyone, especially those we consider to be our enemies. When we show our capacity of listening and understanding, the other person will also listen to us, and we will have a chance to tell them of our pain.

ONE HUNDRED YEARS
FROM NOW

When you are angry with someone you love, breathe mindfully with your eyes closed, and bring your mind to the distant future. Your body and the body of the person with whom you are angry will have dissolved into dust. When we see our lives are so ephemeral, we don't want to waste our time being angry with each other.

EQUANIMITY

Equanimity is an important element of true
love. Some people think equanimity means
indifference. But equanimity isn't cold or indif-
ferent. It means you love without discrimination
and include everyone in your love. It means
seeing the whole situation without taking
sides. When you love because living beings
need your love, not because someone belongs
to your family, your nation, or your religion,
then you are loving without discrimination and
practicing true love.

MINDFUL CLASSROOM, MINDFUL SOCIETY

Many people have enormous suffering and don't know how to handle it. Often it starts at a very young age. If a student is suffering greatly, they can't concentrate and learn. Schools should be places where children can learn to be happy, loving, and understanding, where teachers nourish their students with their own insights and happiness. Very few school programs teach young people how to live—how to deal with anger, reconcile conflicts, how to breathe, smile, and transform difficult feelings. We can transform our classroom into a family where a good relationship can be established between teacher and students. For a child who has difficulties at home, such a teacher and classroom are a second chance. Together we have to create the kinds of public institutions we need for our collective awakening.

BE YOURSELF

To be beautiful means to be yourself. You don't need to be accepted by others. You need to accept yourself. When you are born a lotus flower, be a beautiful lotus flower, don't try to be a magnolia flower. If you crave acceptance and recognition and try to change yourself to fit what other people want you to be, you will suffer all your life. True happiness and true power lie in understanding yourself, accepting yourself, having confidence in yourself.

TWO ASPECTS OF HOPE

Hope is important because it can make the present moment less difficult to bear. If we believe that tomorrow will be better, we can bear a hardship today. But that is the most that hope can do for us. When I think deeply about the nature of hope, I see something tragic: since we cling to our hope for the future, we don't focus our energies and capabilities on the present moment. We use hope to believe something better will happen in the future, that peace will come. Hope becomes a kind of obstacle. If you can refrain from hoping, you can bring yourself entirely into the present moment and discover the joy that is already here.

I don't mean you shouldn't have hope, but that hope is not enough. If you dwell in the energy of hope, you won't bring yourself back entirely into the present moment. If you re-channel that energy into being aware of what is going on in the present moment, you can make a breakthrough and discover joy and peace right in the present moment. The inspirational peace movement leader A.J. Muste said, "There is no way to peace, peace is the way." We can realize peace right in the present moment with our look, our smile, our words, and our actions. Peace work means that each step we make should be peace, joy, and happiness. We can smile and relax. Everything we want is right here in the present moment.

BREATHING AND SMILING
WHEREVER YOU ARE

Our senses are our windows to the world, and sometimes the wind blows through them and disturbs everything within us. Some of us leave our windows open all the time, allowing the sights and sounds of the world to invade and penetrate us.

When you need to slow down and come back to yourself, you don't need to find a special place. Wherever you are, come back and practice conscious breathing. Whether sitting in your office or your car, standing in a busy market, or waiting in line at the bank, if you begin to feel depleted and need to return to yourself, you can practice breathing and smiling.

A COMMUNITY OF PRACTICE

If you throw a rock into the river, no matter how small it is, it will sink to the bottom. But with a boat, you can keep many rocks afloat. If you are alone, you may sink into the river of suffering, but if you have a community of practice and you allow it to embrace your pain and sorrow, you will float. Many of us have profited from the strong collective energy of the sangha.

Imagine you're a drop of water on its way to the ocean. Alone, you might evaporate on the way. But if you allow yourself to be held and transported by the sangha, you go as a river, and you will surely arrive at the ocean. In a sangha, we're like a drop of water in the river. Our pain, sorrow, and suffering are recognized and embraced.

BUILDING BELOVED COMMUNITY

I met the Reverend Martin Luther King, Jr. in
person for the first time in Chicago in 1966.
I could tell I was in the presence of a holy
person. We were both young, both belonged
to the Fellowship of Reconciliation, working
to help groups in conflict find a peaceful
resolution. We had tea together and then went
down to a press conference. This is when Dr.
King spoke out for the first time against the
Vietnam War. We combined our efforts to work
for peace in Vietnam and fight for civil rights
in the US. We agreed that the true enemy of
man is not man, but is the anger, hatred, and
discrimination found in the hearts and minds
of human beings. We met again in 1967 in
Geneva at the Pacem in Terris conference
organized by the World Council of Churches.

There we continued our discussion on peace, freedom, and community. We agreed that without a community, we cannot go very far. Without a happy, harmonious community, we will not be able to realize our dream. I told him, "Martin, in Vietnam they call you a bodhisattva, an enlightened being trying to awaken other living beings." I'm glad I had the chance to tell him, because a few months later he was assassinated. I was in New York when I heard the news. I was devastated. I couldn't eat or sleep. I made a deep vow to continue building the beloved community, not only for myself but for him also. I have done what I promised, and I think that I have always felt his support.

THE COLLECTIVE ENERGY
OF PRACTICE

When we practice together as a group, we
generate a collective energy of mindfulness
and peace that can help heal and nourish
us and our children. Practicing together, we
have the opportunity to produce the powerful,
collective energy of mindfulness, compassion,
concentration, insight, and joy that can help
change the world. We don't need more money,
fame, or wealth in order to be happy. Just by
generating these energies, we can create
freedom and happiness for ourselves and for
many people around us. We have a chance
to be together. Walking from one place to
another, why don't we enjoy every step? We
are here for that. Give yourself pleasure, joy,
and freedom with every step.

EMPTINESS

Emptiness, signlessness, and aimlessness are
keys to unlocking the door of reality. They are
three essential contemplations that liberate us
from our wrong views so we can live deeply
and fully and face dying and death without
fear, anger, or despair. To say that something
is empty does not mean it doesn't exist.
Emptiness doesn't mean nothingness. It means
that something is full of everything except for
one thing: a separate self. The verb "to be"
can be misleading, because we cannot be by
ourselves alone. "To be" is always "to inter-be."
A flower is full of everything in the cosmos. It is
empty of only one thing: a separate existence.
We inter-are with one another and with
all of life.

SIGNLESSNESS

To see a flower only as a flower, and not to see
the sunshine, clouds, earth, time, and space
in it, is to be caught in the sign "flower." When
you touch the interbeing nature of the flower,
you truly see the flower. If you see a person
and don't also see their society, education,
ancestors, culture, and environment, you
haven't really seen that person. Instead, you
have been taken in by the sign of that person,
their outward appearance, the appearance of
being a separate self. When you can see that
person deeply, you touch the whole cosmos
and you will not be fooled by appearances.

AIMLESSNESS

When we put an aim in front of us, we can run
for our whole life, and happiness will never
be possible. Happiness is possible only when
you stop running and cherish the present
moment and who you are. You don't need to
be someone else; you're already a wonder
of life. In the West, we're very goal oriented
and often we forget to enjoy ourselves along
the route. Aimlessness means you don't put
something in front of you and run after it,
because everything is already here, in yourself.
While we practice walking meditation, we don't
try to arrive anywhere. We only make peaceful,
happy steps. If we keep thinking of the future,
of what we want to realize, we will lose our
steps. The same is true with sitting meditation.
We sit just to enjoy our sitting; we don't sit in

order to attain any goal. Each moment of sitting meditation brings us back to life, and we sit in a way that we enjoy our sitting for the entire time we do it. Whether we're eating a tangerine, drinking a cup of tea, or walking in meditation, we should do it in a way that is "aimless."

A COMPASSIONATE SOCIETY

In a civilization where technology is crucial for success, there's little room for compassion. But when we meditate deeply on life, we come to identify even with ants and caterpillars. For society to change, there needs to be a complete change of consciousness. We need to deeply realize the interdependent nature of reality and drop our habitual way of thinking which fragments reality. Continuing to practice the meditation on interdependence, after a while you will notice a change in yourself. Your perspective will widen, and you will find that you look at all living beings with compassion. The grudges and hatreds that you thought were impenetrable will begin to erode, and you will find yourself caring for each and every being. Most important, you will no longer be afraid of life and death.

NON-FEAR

Buddhist texts speak of three kinds of gifts:
material resources; the Dharma (sharing spiritual teachings); and non-fear. Non-fear is the
greatest gift we can offer to others. Nothing
is more precious. But we cannot offer that gift
unless we ourselves have it. If we have prac-
ticed and have touched the ultimate dimension
of reality, we too can smile the bodhisattva's
smile of non-fear. Like them, we don't need to
run away from our afflictions. We don't need to
go somewhere else to attain enlightenment.
We see that afflictions and enlightenment are
one. When we have a deluded mind, we see
only afflictions. But when we have a true mind,
the afflictions are no longer there. There is
only enlightenment. We are no longer afraid
of birth and death because we have touched

the nature of interbeing. Bodhisattvas are free from fear, and they can help many people.

When we realize that afflictions
are no other than enlightenment,
we can ride the waves of birth and death
* in peace.*
Traveling in the boat of compassion
on the ocean of delusion,
smiling the smile of non-fear.

LIKE A CLOUD

While your loved one is still alive and there
with you, be aware that they are like a cloud.
You, too, are a like a cloud and are not entirely
in this body, because every day you produce
thoughts, speech, and actions which continue
independently of you; they are your continuation. Even when the cloud is still in the sky, we
can see its continuation—as rain, snow, or hail.
We must meditate to see that we are not only
in our body, but we are also outside of it. I can
see myself not only in this body, but also in my
friends, my disciples, my work, in many things.
If you want to recognize me, don't look in this
direction; this body is only a small part of me.

I will continue to be.
But you have to be very careful to see me.

I will be a flower, a leaf, or a cloud.
I will be in those forms and send you
   a greeting.
If you are aware enough, you will
   recognize me,
And you will be smiling at me.
I will be very happy.

CONTINUATION

The healing of our body and mind must go together with the healing of the Earth. This kind of enlightenment is crucial for a collective awakening. To be mindful is an act of awakening. We need to wake up to the fact that the earth is in danger, that all living species are in danger. Mindfulness and a deep awareness of the earth can also help us handle pain, difficult feelings and emotions.

Happiness and suffering inter-are. So, we shouldn't be afraid of suffering. We know how to handle it, how to make use of it to build happiness. We speak of the goodness of suffering. This is why we can accept this world with all our heart. We don't need to go anywhere else. This is our home. We want to manifest again and again to make this home more beautiful with good action.

PRACTICES
FOR SMILING

STARTING THE DAY

Waking up this morning, I smile.
Twenty-four brand new hours are before me.
I vow to live fully in each moment
and look at all beings with eyes of compassion.

Every morning, when we wake up, we have
twenty-four brand new hours to live. What
a precious gift! We can live these hours in a
way that brings peace, joy, and happiness to
ourselves and to others. We can smile, breathe,
walk, and eat our meals in a way that allows
us to be in touch with the abundance of happiness that is available. What better way to start
the day than with a smile? Our smile affirms
our awareness and determination to live in
peace and joy. The source of a true smile is an
awakened mind. To remember to smile when

you wake up, you might hang a reminder—such as a branch, a leaf, a painting, or some inspiring words—in your window or from the ceiling above your bed, so you notice it when you wake up. Smiling helps you approach the day with gentleness and understanding.

WALKING MEDITATION

In daily life there's so much to do and so little time. You may feel pressure to run all the time. Just stop. Touch the ground of the present moment deeply, and you will touch real peace and joy. Walking meditation is a wonderful way to come back to ourselves. We walk with grace and dignity. Each step is life.

When walking, keep your breath natural and notice how many steps you take with each in- and out-breath. You may notice your exhalation is longer than your inhalation; maybe you'll take three steps with your in-breath and four steps with your out-breath. When you walk up or downhill, the number of steps per breath will change. Always follow the need of your lungs.

When you're alone, you may like to practice slow walking, taking one step as you breathe in and one step as you breathe out. Focus your attention on the sole of your foot and arrive fully in each step. Walking in a park or in your neighborhood, you can walk in a way that others don't even notice you're practicing. If you meet someone along the way, just smile and continue your walking

We can walk on the planet with as much respect and reverence as we would when walking in any sacred space. Steps like these have the power to save our lives, to rescue us from the state of alienation we're living in and reconnect us with ourselves and the earth. A half-smile will bring calm and delight to your steps and your breath, and help sustain your attention.

PRESENT MOMENT,
WONDERFUL MOMENT

Our breathing is the link between our body and our mind. Sometimes our mind is thinking of one thing and our body is doing another, and mind and body are not unified. By concentrating on our breathing, we bring body and mind back together, and become whole again.

Breathing is a joy I cannot miss. Every day, I practice conscious breathing. I have written in calligraphy the sentence "Breathe, you are alive." and it hangs on the wall in my small meditation room. Just breathing and smiling can make us very happy, because breathing with awareness, we recover ourselves completely and encounter life in the present moment.

In our busy society, it is a great fortune to practice conscious breathing from time to time. We can do this wherever we are, at any time throughout the day. To help us, we can recite these four lines silently as we breathe in and out:

Breathing in, I calm my body.
Breathing out, I smile.
Dwelling in the present moment,
I know this is a wonderful moment!

"Breathing in, I calm my body." Reciting this line is like drinking a glass of cool water on a hot day—you can feel the coolness permeate your body. When I breathe in and recite this line, I actually feel my breath calming my body and mind.

"Breathing out, I smile." You know a smile can relax hundreds of muscles in your face. A smile is a sign that you are master of yourself.

"Dwelling in the present moment." While I

sit here, I don't think of anything else. I know
exactly where I am.

"I know this is a wonderful moment." It is
a joy to sit, stable and at ease, and return to
our breathing, our smiling, our true nature.
Our appointment with life is in the present
moment. If we do not have peace and joy right
now, when will we have peace and joy? What
is preventing us from being happy right now?
As we follow our breathing with our awareness,
we can say silently,

Calming.
Smiling.
Present moment.
Wonderful moment.

DEEP RELAXATION

The practice of deep relaxation is a way to acknowledge, soothe, and heal the suffering in body and mind. Mind and body are not separate. We hold our suffering in our body. When your body is at ease and relaxed, your mind will be at peace as well. You can guide yourself or others in a deep relaxation exercise. A full exercise may take thirty minutes, but five or ten minutes of deep relaxation during a break in the day will relax body and mind. It's important to do some deep relaxation every day.

Lie down on your back (or sit in a chair). Close your eyes. Let your arms rest on either side of your body. Breathing in and out, feel yourself sinking into the floor, letting go of tension, worries, not holding on to anything. Be aware of your abdomen rising and falling as you breathe in and out.

Now we begin observing and releasing the tension in the body. We become aware of each part of our body, from our head to our toes, and bring love and relaxation to each part. For example, "Breathing in, I'm aware of my eyes. Breathing out, I smile to my eyes with gratitude and love." Continue breathing in and out as you take time to care for your eyes. "Breathing in, I'm aware of my shoulders. Breathing out, I allow the tension to flow out into the floor." "Breathing in, I'm aware of my heart. Breathing out, I smile to my heart with love. My heart is essential to my well-being. My heart works nonstop, nourishing all the cells in my body. I'm grateful to my heart, yet I've done things to hurt it. I haven't been kind to my heart." This kind of insight can transform and heal. Bring your awareness to all your organs, all the parts of your body in this way.

If there's a place that's unwell or in pain, send it your love, smile to it, and allow it to rest. Be aware that there are other parts of your body, still strong and healthy, that can help support and heal the weak area.

Once you have finished the body scan, breathe in and out and enjoy the sensation of your whole body, relaxed and calm. Smile to your whole body and send your love and compassion to your whole body.

To end, slowly stretch and open your eyes. Take your time to come to a sitting position, and then to stand up up gently and slowly.

Related Titles by Thich Nhat Hanh

The Art of Living
At Home in the World
Be Free Where You Are
Happiness
The Heart of the Buddha's Teaching
How to Live When a Loved One Dies
Love Letter to the Earth
No Mud, No Lotus
Peace Is Every Step
Present Moment, Wonderful Moment
Reconciliation
The Sun My Heart
Thich Nhat Hanh: Essential Writings
Zen and the Art of Saving the Planet

Further Resources

For information about our international community,
visit: plumvillage.org
To find an online sangha, visit: plumline.org

For more practices and resources, download the
Plum Village app: plumvillage.app

PARALLAX
PRESS

Parallax Press, a nonprofit publisher founded
by Zen Master Thich Nhat Hanh, publishes
books and media on the art of mindful living
and Engaged Buddhism. We are committed to
offering teachings that help transform suffering
and injustice. Our aspiration is to contribute to
collective insight and awakening, bringing about a
more joyful, healthy, and compassionate society.

View our entire library at **parallax.org**.

Monastics and visitors practice the art of mindful living in the tradition of Thich Nhat Hanh at our mindfulness practice centers around the world. To reach any of these communities, or for information about how individuals, couples, and families can join in a retreat, please contact:

Plum Village
33580 Dieulivol, France
plumvillage.org

Magnolia Grove Monastery
Batesville, MS 38606, USA
magnoliagrovemonastery.org

Blue Cliff Monastery
Pine Bush, NY 12566, USA
bluecliffmonastery.org

Deer Park Monastery
Escondido, CA 92026, USA
deerparkmonastery.org

European Institute of Applied Buddhism
D-51545 Waldbröl, Germany
eiab.eu

Thailand Plum Village
Nakhon Ratchasima
30130 Thailand
thaiplumvillage.org

Healing Spring Monastery
77510 Verdelot,
France
healingspringmonastery.org

Maison de l'Inspir
77510 Villeneuve-sur-Bellot
France
maisondelinspir.org

Asian Institute of Applied Buddhism
Ngong Ping, Lantau Island
Hong Kong
pvfhk.org

Nhap Luu-Stream Entering Monastery
Porcupine Ridge, Victoria 3461
Australia
nhapluu.org

Mountain Spring Monastery
Bilpin, Victoria 2758
Australia
mountainspringmonastery.org

The Mindfulness Bell, a journal of the art of mindful living in the tradition of Thich Nhat Hanh, is published two times a year by our community. To subscribe or to see the world-wide directory of sanghas (local mindfulness groups), visit **mindfulnessbell.org**.